BASIC INGREDIENTS

THE
MUSHROOM
COOKBOOK

BASIC INGREDIENTS

THE
MUSHROOM
COOKBOOK

MORE THAN SIXTY
EASY, IMAGINATIVE RECIPES

EDITED BY
NICOLA HILL

COURAGE
BOOKS

AN IMPRINT OF
RUNNING PRESS BOOK PUBLISHERS

Philadelphia • London

Canadian representatives:
General Publishing Co., Ltd.,
30 Lesmill Road, Don Mills, Ontario M3B 2T6.

10 9 8 7 6 5 4 3
Digit on the right indicates the number of this printing
Library of Congress Cataloguing in Publication Number 94-67591

ISBN 1-56138-491-7
Printed in Singapore

Reprinted 1995

Acknowledgements
Commissioning Editor: Nicola Hill
Editors: Isobel Holland & Jo Lethaby
U.S. Consultant: Jenni Fleetwood
Art Editors: Meryl James & Sue Michniewicz
Production Controller: Sasha Judelson
Photographer: Nick Carman
Home Economist: Jennie Shapter
Stylist: Jane McLeish
Illustrator: Roger Gorringe/Garden Studio
Information on cultivated mushrooms supplied by Victoria
Lloyd-Davies; and wild mushrooms by Dr. David Pegler

This edition published in the United States of America in 1995
by Courage Books
an imprint of Running Press Book Publishers
125 South Twenty-Second Street
Philadelphia, PA 19103-4399

Notes
Warning: Collected wild mushrooms should always be shown to,
and approved by, an experienced mushroom collector. **Never** eat
any mushroom where there is any doubt in recognizing the species.

Microwave methods are based on microwave ovens
with a High Power output of 800 watts.

All the jellies, jams and preserves should be processed in a boiling
water-bath canner according to the U.S.D.A. guidelines.

CONTENTS

Collecting Wild Mushrooms

*First learn to recognize the poisonous species.

*Always collect mushrooms in baskets or cotton bags, NEVER in plastic bags.

*Do not mix different species.

*Do not collect mushrooms after prolonged heavy rains. Mushrooms, soaked in rainwater, quickly lose both color and form.

*Do not collect young mushrooms, unless mature examples are also present. They are difficult to recognize as they lack the characteristic appearance of the mature mushroom. Similarly, do not collect old, decaying specimens.

*Collected mushrooms should be shown to and approved by an experienced mushroom collector.

*Contaminated mushrooms such as those with mold or ones collected near roadsides, can result in food poisoning.

*Species not previously tried before should only be eaten in small quantities.

Buying and Cooking Mushrooms

*Buy mushrooms often and in small quantities.

*Eat mushrooms as fresh as possible.

*Store mushrooms in the refrigerator, in a paper bag or wrapped in paper towels. Do not wash before storing and handle as little as possible.

*There is no need to soak or peel cultivated mushrooms. The skin contains valuable nutrients. Simply brush off any peat or rinse quickly in a colander under cold running water. However, it is best to soak wild mushrooms to remove any grit.

*While all cultivated mushrooms can be eaten raw, most people prefer to cook larger varieties. Cook mushrooms quickly to seal in their flavors, or add them to casseroles, for the last 20 minutes of cooking.

*Do not remove the stems from cultivated mushrooms, although if advised do remove them from wild mushrooms. If a recipe requires that stems are removed, do so but cut the stems flush with the gills.

*Mushrooms can be cooked by almost any method, from the barbecue to the microwave.

Mushroom Nutrition

Mushrooms are nutritious. They contain few calories and no cholesterol. Mushroom protein is superior to other vegetable proteins because of its essential amino acid content. The white mushroom *(Agaricus bisporus)* ranks above all other vegetables, except beans, peas and lentils, in its amino acid content. Mushrooms are easily digestible and contain vitamins B12, folic acid and minerals, particularly potassium.

Cep – (*Boletus edulis*) – wild
This is an excellent edible mushroom. It has a robust, firm mushroom cap, is found on the ground in the autumn in pine, oak and chestnut woods. The smooth cap can grow up to 7 inches across, it is strongly convex in form and colored light brown to bronze. Under the cap the whitish surface is flat and covered with minute pores, each of which forms the opening to a vertical tube. The stem is thick with a fine white network pattern on the upper surface. This is a good species however cooked, with a delicate flavor. The mushrooms are frequently dried on strings and used in soups after soaking, or pickled.

Cep

Chanterelle – (*Cantharellus cibarius*) – wild
This striking pale orange to egg-yolk yellow mushroom is generally found amongst mosses under beech and oak trees, from June to October. It is also known under the name of "Girolle." The depressed cap has a wavy, inrolled margin, and the more brightly colored underside bears thick, well-spaced ridges. It has a strong odor of apricots, which can be retained by gentle cooking. The mushrooms are also suitable for drying and pickling. It is one of the most popular of the edible mushrooms.

Chestnut mushroom – (*Agaricus brunnescens*) – cultivated
These are similar to the cultivated white mushrooms, but the strain is slightly different, producing a mushroom with a brown outer skin, a firm texture and a stronger, more nutty flavor. Chestnut mushrooms have a higher percentage of dry matter so they are excellent in pâtés, breads and pastries. These mushrooms are picked and sold at two stages of their growth — closed caps which are round with closed veils, and flats which are larger with the dark brown gills clearly visible.

Chestnut mushroom

Crimini Mushrooms (*Agaricus Brunnescens*)
Crimini mushrooms are also known as Italian or Roman Brown mushrooms. They are light tan to dark brown in color with a deep earthy flavor. Their meaty, rich flavor is more intense than the white mushroom. Crimini mushrooms are excellent with beef, in stir-fries and vegetable sautés.

Enoki-take – (*Flammulina velutipes*) – cultivated and wild
Enoki mushrooms have long thin stems joined at the base, with a tiny button mushroom at the top of each stem. Only trim off the base; both the stems and the caps are edible. Enoki mushrooms should be eaten raw.

They have a light, mild flavor and crisp texture. Toss them into salads, tuck into sandwiches and use as a garnish for soups.

Fairy Ring Champignon – (*Marasmius oreades*) – wild
This is a small mushroom, much despised by ardent gardeners for it forms fairy rings on lawns which can persist for years. The small, buffy brown, smooth cap grows up to 2 inches across and has a raised center, whereas the underside has widely spaced, off-white gills. As it is a thin-fleshed species, it is normally used in the preparation of soups and gravies. It has, too, the advantage of being dried easily. When picking, care must be taken to avoid the "Cream Clot" (*Clitocybe dealbata*) which is poisonous.

Fairy Ring Champignon

Field Mushroom – (*Agaricus campestris*) – wild
A true mushroom, found in fields and open grassland. It resembles the "Cultivated Mushroom," with a white to pale brown cap, 1-4 inches across. The underlying gills are at first bright pink, becoming progressivly dark brown as the mushroom ages. The short, stem has a small, membranous ring attached to it. When the mushroom is broken open, the white flesh quickly discolors to pink. This mushroom has a nutty flavor.

Field Mushroom

Giant Puffball – (*Langermannia gigantea*) – wild
This is probably the easiest of all the fungi to recognize. It forms a large, ball-shaped cap, 20 inches or more across. The surface is at first white then discolors to brown as it eventually breaks up and flakes away. The flesh is firm and white at first before becoming brown. These mushrooms are not always common but in certain years they may be found in large numbers, when they can form fairy rings in open woodland, grassland or on disturbed soil. The flesh is delicious when gently fried in butter, but may only be eaten when it is firm and white.

Honey Fungus – (*Armillaria mellea*) – wild
This is the mushroom found growing in large clusters throughout the late fall at the base of tree trunks. The yellowish-brown caps, 1-4 inches across, have tiny, black, fibrous scales, the gills are whitish but soon discolor with reddish spots, and the fibrous stem bears a white, cottony ring. The mushrooms should always be cooked, and it is best to eat only the young specimens.

Horn of Plenty – (*Craterellus cornucopioides*) – wild
A wild mushroom which has been collected for consumption

for many years. In France it is known as "*la viande des pauvres*" and is also known as "Black Trumpets," which best describes its appearance. Although not common they can be abundant in certain areas, growing amongst leaf litter in beech and oak woods. The cap forms a grayish-black, conical shape, with a hollow center and lacking mushroom-type gills. There is little or no stem. The flesh provides a good flavor and texture, and is used in casseroles.

Horn of Plenty

Horse Mushroom – (*Agaricus arvensis*) – wild
A large, white mushroom growing in open grassland. The cap may be convex or flattened, growing up to 6 inches across, and remains smooth or becomes very slightly scaly. Underneath the cap, the crowded gills change from grayish to dark chocolate-brown. The white, cylindrical stem bears a large, membranous ring on the upper region. Fresh specimens have a smell of bitter almonds or aniseed which may just be retained after cooking. When collecting, care must be taken to avoid the poisonous, "Yellow-staining Mushroom" (*Agaricus xanthodermus*), which grows in hedgerows, has a large, fleshy ring and, most importantly, when the base of the stem is broken open the flesh immediately turns yellow.

***Auricularia - (auricula-judae)* – wild**
A strange-looking mushroom, which grows on the branches of several species of tree, particularly elder and sycamore, during late fall. The mushroom is gelatinous to the touch, ear-shaped and grows up to 1-4 inches across. The outer surface is reddish-brown to blackish, and the underside is irregularly ridged. There is no stem. These mushrooms are widely used in Chinese cuisine.

Auricularia

Matsutake – (*Tricholoma matsutake*) – wild
This is a mushroom which grows wild but only in Japan, with a closely related form found in the conifer forests of northwestern America. The cap, up to 5 inches across, soon becomes flattened and covered with small, reddish-brown scales. The stem is also covered with soft, brown scales below a white ring, and the gills are white and crowded. This is a much prized mushroom in Japanese cuisine.

Morel – (*Morchella esculenta*) – wild
Morels appear in late spring, in orchards and woods, under hedgerows or on open waste-

land. The mushrooms, about 1-3 inches across, have a distinctive appearance. The head is ovoid to conical, yellowish-brown in color, and bears branching, deep ridges which give a honeycomb-like appearance. The stem is about 1 inch thick, scurfy white and hollow. It is prized as a food although it must be cooked first. Care must be taken to avoid the "False Morel" *(Gyromitra esculenta)*, which is poisonous.

Morel

Orange Peel Fungus – (*Aleuria aurantiaca*) – wild
The mushrooms appear as bright orange cups, 1-2½ inches across, with a brittle flesh and devoid of a stem. The outer surface is off-white and scurfy. The mushroom may be found from May to October on hard or disturbed soil.

Oyster Mushroom – (*Pleurotus ostreatus*) – cultivated and wild
Also referred to as Pleurottes, Pleurotes or Pleurotus, oyster mushrooms are beige, cream or gray in color with fluted caps that resemble an oyster shell or fan. Oyster mushrooms have a delicate flavor and soft texture. All Oyster mushrooms are best eaten young and have a delicate texture and flavor so they should only be cooked for a short period. They are better steamed and should be served with chicken, seafood, veal, pork or vegetable dishes and are ideal for stir-fries.

Oyster

Padi Straw Mushroom – (*Volvariella volvacea*) – wild and cultivated
A species which is widely cultivated and eaten throughout Southeast Asia. It grows on sawdust or decaying straw. The yellowish-brown conical cap grows to about 2 inches across and appears streaky, the gills are white then pink, and the solid stem is white. It is charac-terized by at first being enclosed within a fleshy veil or skin when young, and this is the stage most often encountered in Chinese cooking.

Parasol Mushroom - (*Macrolepiota procera*) - wild
This is one of the largest, most conspicuous and possibly the best of the wild, edible mush-rooms. It appears from late summer and continues through the fall months, growing in grassland or on hedge-banks. The caps may expand up to 9 inches or more, but the young closed caps are round, borne upon a tall stem. The cap retains a raised central region, and is covered with shaggy, brown scales, the gills are white and crowded, and the stem may be up to 16 inches and is covered with zig-zag scales. There is a large, movable ring

in the upper region. The thick, white flesh is firm, and has a smell of newly ground meal. It is the sliced caps which are normally eaten. In the southern states of North America, care must be taken not to confuse this species with the "Green-spored Lepiota" *(Chlorophyllum molybdites),* which is poisonous.

Parasol Mushroom

Shaggy Ink Caps – *(Coprinus comatus)* – wild
This mushroom, which is also widely known as the "Lawyer's Wig," can be found in fields from spring through to late fall. The gills blacken and dissolve

into a black ink. The cap is tall, up to 5 inches, cylindrical, whitish, and covered with large, recurved scales. The stem grows up to 4-5 inches and is fibrous, with a small, movable ring. It is best to pick the young specimens in the early morning as they contain a great deal less water and therefore have a much better flavor.

Shiitake – *(Lentinula edodes)* – cultivated
Also referred to as Oak, Chinese or Black Forest mushrooms, they are tan to dark brown in color with a large open, white veil on the under side, between the cap and the stem. Unlike other mushrooms, the stem should be trimmed off — only use the cap for cooking. These mushrooms have a full-bodied, meaty flavor with a spongy texture when cooked. Sauté in butter with garlic, add to soups, stir-fries, pastas and meat dishes. Originally from the Far East, this mushroom is perfectly suited to spicy Asian recipes.

St George's – *(Calocybe gambosa)* – wild
One of the few wild, edible mushrooms available in the spring, from April through to June. The caps grow up

to 6 inches across, are thick and irregularly convex, cream-colored or with gray to reddish tints. The underlying gills are white and densely crowded, and the stem is robust, whitish and usually thickened toward the base. They have a distinctive smell and taste of newly ground meal, and may be eaten fresh or after drying when the flavor is retained. They are usually cut into pieces and cooked with meat, enhancing their natural flavor.

St George's.

Summer Truffle – *(Tuber aestivum)* – wild
A truffle is a fungus which grows under the ground. The famous White Piedmont Truffle

(Tuber magnatum), from Italy, is the world's most expensive food. The summer truffle is a widespread species. It forms a small, hard ball about 1-3 inches across, black, covered with prominent wart-like scales. Inside, the flesh is finely marbled with white veins. The flavor of truffles is excellent, with a pleasant smell and a nutty taste. As truffles are expensive, sprinkle a little chopped truffle into an omelet.

White mushrooms - *(Agaricus bisporus)* - cultivated

The common white or button mushroom is available in three different sizes - small, medium and large. These mushrooms range from white to light brown in color. They have an extremely mild flavor which intensifies greatly when cooked. Those white mushrooms with open veils, known as stuffers, are more mature with a richer taste. The white mushroom is extremely versatile.

SMALL MUSHROOMS are light and delicate in flavor and are best eaten raw with dips, in salads or lightly marinated. They are also a good addition to soups, stir-fries and pasta dishes or you could sauté them to top meat or poultry.

Closed Cup Mushroom

MEDIUM MUSHROOMS have a stronger flavor than the small mushroom and are ideal for use in stir-fries, on pizzas and with pasta or rice. Again, use them in dishes and sauces which are light and pale in color.

LARGE MUSHROOMS are the perfect choice for making garlic mushrooms. They are also excellent for use in pies and casseroles and to serve as a vegetable to accompany meat and game.

STUFFERS often have a superb flavor and are ideal for serving whole or in soups and sauces. They also work well as a vegetable accompaniment, to be served with broiled steak or bacon and eggs.

Wood Blewit - *(Lepista nuda)* - wild

Wood Blewits may be found during the fall and winter months, growing amongst the leaf litter. The caps range from 2-6 inches across, and are dark brown to purplish-lilac, with a smooth, shiny surface, and the thick stem is also tinged with violet. The gills are sometimes violaceous but turn a dirty flesh pink color. The flavor is strong. It is recommended that mushrooms should first be boiled. Some individuals have an allergic reaction to this species. Care must be taken not to confuse this species with *Cortinarius alboviolaceus.*

Wood Blewit

WILD MUSHROOM SOUP

Serves 4-6

1 tablespoon corn oil
¾ pound wild mushrooms, rinsed, trimmed and
cut into strips or chopped (*about 3 cups*)
½ onion, chopped
1 bunch watercress, chopped
½ garlic clove, crushed
4 cups chicken or vegetable stock
1 tablespoon coarsely chopped fresh parsley
2 egg yolks
2 tablespoons heavy cream

Heat the corn oil in a saucepan. Add the wild
mushrooms and chopped onion and sauté
gently for 5 minutes. Add the watercress,
garlic and chicken or vegetable stock to the
pan and simmer gently over a low heat for
20 minutes.

Add the chopped parsley, mixing well. Beat
the egg yolks with the heavy cream. Add a
little soup to the cream, then stir into the soup
and cook gently to thicken but do not let boil.
Serve hot.

MUSHROOM & HAZELNUT SOUP

Serves 4

¼ stick butter
3 cups sliced medium mushrooms
¼ cup ground hazelnuts
2½ cups vegetable or chicken stock
2 cups milk
¼ teaspoon ground nutmeg
3 tablespoons light cream
salt and freshly ground black pepper

Melt the butter in a large saucepan, add the
mushrooms and stir over a medium heat for
2-3 minutes, until the juices run. Put the lid
on the pan and simmer gently in the juices
for 5 minutes. Take out 2 tablespoons of the
mushrooms and reserve for garnishing later.

Stir the hazelnuts into the mushrooms in the
pan, then add the stock, milk and nutmeg, and
season to taste. Cover the pan and simmer
gently for 10 minutes.

Process the soup in a blender or food
processor until smooth. Return to the rinsed
out pan, stir in the cream and the reserved
cooked mushrooms and reheat gently until
piping hot but not boiling. Adjust the
seasoning to taste, and serve.

Illustrated opposite

CHINESE MUSHROOM SOUP

Serves 4

**6 dried Chinese mushrooms,
or ¼ pound fresh large open mushrooms
(*field mushrooms, if available*)
2 teaspoons cornstarch
1 tablespoon cold water
3 egg whites
2 teaspoons salt
2½ cups chicken or vegetable stock
freshly ground black pepper
finely chopped scallions, for garnish**

Soak the dried mushrooms in warm water for 20-30 minutes, then squeeze dry, discard the hard stems and slice thinly. If using fresh mushrooms, rinse and slice them.

Mix the cornstarch with the water. Comb the egg whites with your fingers to loosen them (do not use a whisk as too much air will make them frothy) and add a pinch of the salt.

Bring the stock to a boil in a saucepan and add the mushrooms. Simmer for 5 minutes, then add the cornstarch, stirring constantly, until slightly thickened.

Add the remaining salt and pour the egg white very slowly into the soup, stirring all the time. Adjust seasoning if necessary. Garnish with the scallions and serve hot.

MUSHROOM & WILD RICE SOUP

Serves 6

**½ ounce dried wild mushrooms
1 cup boiling water
⅓ cup wild rice
½ cup chopped onions
2 tablespoons olive oil
1-2 garlic cloves, crushed
2 cups chopped large mushrooms
1 teaspoon dried thyme
1 bay leaf
4 cups cold water
salt and freshly ground black pepper**

Cover dried mushrooms with the boiling water and soak for 20 minutes. Drain and reserve soaking water. Rinse mushrooms, then chop. Strain soaking water through strainer lined with paper towels. Set mushrooms and soaking water aside.

Put the wild rice in a saucepan of salted cold water and bring to a boil. Cover and simmer gently for 40 minutes or until tender.

Meanwhile, sauté the onions in the oil in another pan until a rich brown color. Add garlic and cook 30 seconds, add fresh and dried mushrooms with their soaking water, the herbs and the cold water. Bring to a boil, cover and simmer for 15 minutes. Discard bay leaf. Drain rice, add to soup, season to taste and serve hot.

MUSHROOM & SHERRY PATE

Serves 6

½ stick butter or margarine
6 cups thinly sliced small mushrooms
3 tablespoons heavy cream
1 tablespoon dry sherry
6-8 slices whole wheat bread
salt and freshly ground black pepper

Heat half the butter in a large saucepan and, keeping the heat high, sauté half the mushrooms quickly for 3-4 minutes, until just tender and lightly browned. If they begin to make liquid, the butter is not hot enough – the mushrooms should be dry. Remove with a slotted spoon and set aside. Repeat with remaining butter and mushrooms. Remove six perfect mushroom slices and reserve for the garnish. Work the rest in a blender or food processor with the cream, sherry and seasoning to taste. Spoon the mixture into six individual ramekins or pâté dishes, level the tops, then press one of the reserved mushroom slices into the top of each. Cool, then chill the pâtés.

Use the bread to make Melba toast. Toast the bread on both sides, then with a sharp knife cut through the bread to split each slice in half, making two thin pieces. Toast the uncooked sides under the broiler until crisp and brown – the edges will curl up. Let the toast cool. It will keep for 2-3 days in an airtight tin.

CHICKEN LIVER & MUSHROOM PATE

Serves 4

2 bacon slices, chopped
1 onion, chopped
1 garlic clove, crushed
1 cup sliced medium mushrooms
½ pound chicken livers, cleaned
and coarsely chopped
fresh thyme sprig, or pinch of dried
1 bay leaf
1 stick butter
1-2 tablespoons brandy
3 tablespoons fresh green peppercorns
in brine (*optional*, *see page 30*)
salt

Sauté bacon, onion, garlic, mushrooms, livers and herbs in half the butter for 10 minutes until cooked. Discard the bay leaf. Spoon into a blender or food processor with the pan juices and brandy and blend until smooth.

Stir in 2 tablespoons of the peppercorns, if using, and add salt to taste. Spoon into a 2-cup serving dish and smooth the top.

Clarify remaining butter by heating it until it foams, then strain through cheesecloth. Sprinkle remaining peppercorns over pâté and pour over melted clarified butter. Refrigerate until set, then serve with toast.

EGG & MUSHROOM SALAD

Serves 4

3 tablespoons lemon juice
3 cups small mushrooms
2 teaspoons ground cumin
or dried tarragon (*optional*)
1 crisp lettuce, cut into thick slices
⅔ cup cultured buttermilk
or plain yogurt
2 hard-boiled eggs, finely chopped
freshly ground black pepper

Put the lemon juice in a bowl and thinly slice the mushrooms directly into the lemon juice to prevent discoloration. Add the cumin or tarragon, if using, and toss well. Drain, reserving any juice.

Divide the lettuce slices among four plates. Spoon the mushrooms on top, then mix the lemon juice left in the bowl with the buttermilk or yogurt and the chopped eggs. Spoon the mixture over the mushrooms.

Sprinkle each salad generously with black pepper and let stand for 15 minutes before serving, to allow the flavors to blend.

MUSHROOM & TOMATO SALAD

Serves 8

2 cups small mushrooms, halved
¼ pound oyster mushrooms
⅔ cup French dressing
2 tablespoons chopped fresh mint
½ pound tiny cherry tomatoes, halved

Put all the mushrooms in a dish. Combine the French dressing with the chopped mint and pour it over the mushrooms. Cover the dish tightly and leave to marinate for at least 3-4 hours, turning occasionally.

Drain the excess dressing (but not the mint) and arrange the mushrooms in a serving bowl. Add the tomatoes and serve.

Illustrated opposite

CHICORY SALAD WITH MUSHROOMS

Serves 4

1 head chicory
2 cups sliced mushrooms
1 slice (*about 2 ounces*) cooked ham,
cut into small strips
1 small fennel bulb, washed and thinly sliced
10 cherry tomatoes, halved
dill sprigs, for garnish

DRESSING:

¼ cup tomato juice
2 tablespoons lemon juice
1 tablespoon chopped fresh parsley,
chives or mint
salt and freshly ground black pepper

To make the dressing, whisk the tomato juice with the lemon juice. Stir in the chopped herbs. Season to taste with salt and freshly ground black pepper. Mix well.

Cut the stem from the chicory, separate the leaves, wash and drain well.

Put the mushrooms in a salad bowl. Add the dressing and toss until all the mushrooms are coated. Leave to marinate for 30 minutes.

Add the cooked ham, fennel, tomatoes and chicory to the mushrooms. Toss well before serving the salad, garnished with dill.

MUSHROOM & BLUE CHEESE SALAD

Serves 4

2 cups sliced medium mushrooms
1 tablespoon snipped fresh chives
1 tablespoon grated Parmesan cheese

DRESSING:

3 ounces dolcelatte or other creamy blue cheese
¼ cup plain yogurt
1 teaspoon pesto
salt and freshly ground black pepper

Put the sliced mushrooms into a bowl with the snipped chives.

Put the cheese into a blender or food processor with the yogurt and pesto, and season to taste; blend until smooth.

Stir the dressing into the mushrooms, taking care not to spoil their shape. Sprinkle with grated Parmesan.

BROCCOLI & MUSHROOM SALAD

Serves 4

¾ pound broccoli spears
2½ cups thinly sliced small or
medium mushrooms
1 tablespoon walnut halves

DRESSING:

½ cup plain yogurt
1 tablespoon olive oil
1 tablespoon lemon juice
salt and freshly ground black pepper

Cut the broccoli spears into even-size pieces, about 1-inch in length. Cook in salted boiling water for a few minutes until just tender. Drain and cool.

For the dressing, mix together the yogurt, oil, lemon juice and seasoning.

Toss the broccoli and mushrooms together and pour on the dressing. Toss lightly and sprinkle with the walnuts.

Serve cold, but preferably not chilled – the salad improves if left to stand at room temperature for at least 20 minutes before serving.

MUSHROOM SALAD

Serves 8

3 cups baby button mushrooms
2 large garlic cloves, crushed
3 tablespoons finely chopped fresh parsley
3 tablespoons finely snipped fresh chives
3 scallions, sliced
grated rind and juice of 2 lemons
salt and freshly ground black pepper
parsley sprigs, for garnish

Put all the mushrooms into a large bowl. Add the rest of the ingredients. Season lightly and turn with a spoon.

Cover closely and store in the refrigerator for 24 hours before serving the mushrooms, garnished with parsley sprigs.

MUSHROOM, SPINACH & HAZELNUT SALAD

Serves 4

**6 ounces young fresh spinach leaves,
washed and shaken**
½ cup sliced small or medium mushrooms
½ cup sliced chestnut mushrooms
½ cup coarsely chopped hazelnuts

DRESSING:

2 tablespoons olive oil
2 tablespoons white wine vinegar
1 garlic clove, chopped
2 tablespoons coarsely chopped fresh parsley
2 tablespoons plain yogurt
salt and freshly ground black pepper

To make the dressing, put the olive oil, wine vinegar, garlic, parsley, yogurt and seasoning to taste, into a blender or food processor and blend until smooth.

Tear the spinach leaves into pieces and place in a large serving bowl. Scatter the mushrooms and hazelnuts over the spinach. Spoon the prepared dressing over the salad, and toss lightly.

Illustrated on jacket

AVOCADO & MUSHROOM SALAD

Serves 4

2 cups small button mushrooms, quartered
½ head chicory
1 lime or small lemon
3 avocados
¼ cup pignoli (*pine nuts*), toasted
grated rind of ½ lemon

DRESSING:

⅓ cup olive oil
3-4 tablespoons lime juice
1 garlic clove, crushed
1 teaspoon crushed coriander seeds
1 teaspoon honey
salt and freshly ground black pepper

Mix the dressing ingredients together and season to taste. Put the mushrooms in a large bowl, pour over the dressing and toss well, until all the mushrooms are coated.

Arrange chicory in a serving bowl. Squeeze the juice from half the lime or lemon; slice the remainder. Slice the avocados, sprinkle with lime or lemon juice to prevent discoloration and arrange on top of the chicory. Spoon the mushrooms into the center. Sprinkle over the pignoli and lemon rind and garnish with the lime or lemon slices. Serve immediately.

Illustrated opposite

MUSHROOM & GRUYERE SALAD

Serves 4

½ pound Gruyère cheese,
cut into small cubes (*about 2 cups*)
1 cup medium mushrooms, quartered
4 large lettuce leaves
1 tablespoon finely chopped fresh parsley,
for garnish

DRESSING:

¼ cup olive oil
2 tablespoons red wine vinegar
1 garlic clove, crushed
½ teaspoon salt
large pinch of freshly ground black pepper

Put all the dressing ingredients in a screw-top jar and shake until well mixed.

Place the cubes of Gruyère and the quartered mushrooms in a mixing bowl and pour over the prepared dressing. Toss to coat and leave for 20 minutes.

Line a shallow salad bowl with the lettuce leaves. Spoon the cheese mixture on top of the lettuce and sprinkle with the chopped parsley. Serve at once.

CURRIED MUSHROOMS

Serves 4

3 cups sliced medium mushrooms
chopped fresh parsley, for garnish

DRESSING:

3 tablespoons plain yogurt
2 tablespoons chutney
3 tablespoons mayonnaise
1 teaspoon curry powder
salt and freshly ground black pepper

For the dressing, mix together in a bowl the yogurt, chutney, mayonnaise and curry powder, and season to taste.

Add the mushrooms and mix well. Arrange in a serving dish and chill for at least 2 hours before serving, garnished with the chopped fresh parsley.

MUSHROOMS A LA GRECQUE

Serves 4

2 tablespoons olive oil
1 onion, chopped
1 tablespoon tomato paste
⅔ cup dry white wine
2 tablespoons lemon juice
1 teaspoon coriander seeds, crushed
1 parsley sprig
1 thyme sprig
1 small celery stalk with leaves
1 bay leaf
½ pound medium mushrooms
salt and freshly ground black pepper
½ head chicory, to serve

Heat the oil in a skillet, add the onion and cook for 5 minutes. Stir in the tomato paste, wine, lemon juice, coriander seeds, parsley, thyme, celery, bay leaf and seasoning and bring to a boil.

Add the mushrooms to the pan and simmer for 5 minutes over a gentle heat. Remove from the heat, cover and let cool completely in the liquid – about 2-3 hours.

Discard the parsley, thyme, celery stalk and bay leaf. Arrange a bed of chicory leaves in a shallow serving dish. Spoon the chilled mushrooms and the liquid into the center and serve with crusty French bread.

SWEET BLACK MUSHROOMS

Serves 4

15 dried shiitake mushrooms, with large caps
2 cups water
1½ teaspoons sugar
1-2 tablespoons mirin (*sweet rice wine*)
pinch of salt
2 teaspoons shoyu (*Japanese soy sauce*)
FOR GARNISH:
shredded scallions
carrot slices

Soak the dried mushrooms in warm water for 25 minutes. Drain, reserving the soaking liquid, then discard the stems. Leave the caps whole or slice each one into five pieces.

Pour the mushroom liquid slowly into a saucepan, taking care to avoid including the sandy sediment at the bottom which should be discarded. Add the mushrooms and boil for 5 minutes. Add the remaining ingredients and cook for 5 minutes; if liked, sprinkle in a little more mirin.

Remove from the heat and let stand for 10 minutes. Arrange the mushrooms on a serving plate. Garnish with the shredded scallions and carrot slices. Serve at room temperature as a side dish.

MINI STUFFED MUSHROOMS

Serves 8-10

50 small mushrooms suitable for stuffing
1 cup diced Camembert, Brie
or Cambozola cheese
½ stick butter, softened
1 cup finely chopped walnut pieces
2 garlic cloves, crushed
2 tablespoons fresh parsley, chopped
a little milk

Trim the stems off the mushrooms level with the gills. Chop the stems and put into a bowl with the diced cheese (including any rind), butter, walnuts, garlic, parsley and a little milk. Beat all the ingredients together until well mixed but firm.

Place the mushrooms, stem side up, in a large shallow ovenproof dish or pizza dish. Put a spoonful of the walnut mixture on top of each mushroom, dividing it among them.

Place the mushrooms in a preheated oven, 400°F, and bake for about 8-10 minutes, or until the mushrooms are just tender, and serve as an appetizer.

MUSHROOM KABOBS

Serves 12

36 medium mushrooms
1 sweet red or green sweet pepper, seeded and
cut into 1 x ½-inch pieces
24 pearl onions
12 baby zucchini, about ¾ pound, cut into
¾-inch thick slices
MARINADE:
3 tablespoons Dijon mustard
3 garlic cloves, crushed
3 tablespoons dark brown sugar
3 tablespoons soy sauce
3 tablespoons olive oil
1½ teaspoons salt
freshly ground black pepper

Thread the vegetables onto 12 skewers: first a mushroom, then a piece of pepper, an onion, and a zucchini slice. Continue until skewers are full. Lay them flat on a large plate.

Mix together marinade ingredients and spoon over the kabobs making sure all the vegetables are coated. Leave to marinate for at least 1 hour, basting occasionally. Cook kabobs on a barbecue or under a hot broiler 10-15 minutes, until tender. Serve on a bed of rice, with any remaining marinade in a small pitcher.

Illustrated opposite

24

PIZZA MUSHROOMS

Serves 4

1 tablespoon olive oil
2 garlic cloves, quartered
1 teaspoon freshly ground coriander
12 fresh green peppercorns in brine
(*see page 30*)
5 ripe tomatoes, peeled, seeded and chopped
1 can (*2 ounces*) anchovy fillets,
drained and chopped
20 medium mushrooms, about
2-inches in diameter
¾ cup shredded Edam cheese
1 cup fresh brown bread crumbs
20 capers
salt and coarsely ground black pepper

Heat the oil, cook the garlic with the coriander, green peppercorns and salt and pepper for 1-2 minutes. Add the tomatoes and cook until soft. Add one-fourth of the anchovies, stir, remove from the heat and cool slightly.

Trim the stems off the mushrooms level with the gills. Mix the cheese and bread crumbs together. Arrange the mushrooms, stems up, in a broiler pan.

Spread tomato mixture over each mushroom. Place a caper and a piece of anchovy on each one and top with the bread crumb mixture. Place under a preheated medium hot broiler until crisp and sizzling. Serve warm or cold.

MUSHROOM TERRINE

Serves 6

1¼ pounds firm cèpes or large
stuffing mushrooms
¼ cup olive oil
1 pound sausage meat
2 garlic cloves, crushed
2 tablespoons chopped fresh parsley
½ teaspoon dried thyme
1 cup fresh white bread crumbs
milk, for soaking
6 slices of ham
salt and freshly ground black pepper

Trim stems from mushrooms and chop stems finely. Heat half the oil in a saucepan. Add mushroom stems and cook 2-3 minutes. Add sausage, garlic, parsley and thyme. Stir over a moderate heat until lightly browned.

Meanwhile, soak the bread crumbs in a little milk. Squeeze out any excess milk and add to the sausage mixture, mixing well.

Line a greased ovenproof dish with two slices of ham. Top with a little of the sausage mixture and a layer of mushrooms. Continue layering in this way, seasoning between each layer, finishing with a layer of overlapping mushrooms. Sprinkle with the remaining oil. Cover and bake in a preheated oven, 425°F, for 30 minutes. Serve hot.

MUSHROOM & NUT LOAF

Serves 6

2 tablespoons corn oil
1½ cups chopped onions
2 cups chopped medium or large mushrooms
2 cups coarsely ground Brazil nuts
2 cups fresh whole wheat bread crumbs
1 egg
2 teaspoons Worcestershire sauce
salt and freshly ground black pepper

Heat the corn oil in a large saucepan. Add the chopped onions and sauté, stirring frequently, for 5 minutes. Add the mushrooms and sauté for 5 minutes more.

Remove the pan from the heat and stir in the Brazil nuts and bread crumbs.

Beat the egg with the Worcestershire sauce and seasoning and add to the mushroom and nut mixture. Mix well. Press the mixture into a lightly greased 7 x 3-inch loaf pan.

Bake in a preheated oven, 350°F, for 1 hour, or until the loaf is lightly browned. Remove from the pan and serve hot. Alternatively, if serving cold, cool in the pan before inverting onto a platter.

FENNEL WITH MUSHROOMS

Serves 4

2 heads fennel, each about 10 ounces,
trimmed and quartered lengthwise
1 cup thickly sliced medium mushrooms
1 tablespoon lemon juice
2 tablespoons water
1 teaspoon sugar
1 tablespoon finely chopped fresh parsley
¼ stick butter
salt and freshly ground black pepper
fennel leaves, for garnish

Cook the fennel quarters in salted boiling water to cover for 5-6 minutes until almost tender. Drain well.

Arrange the pieces of fennel in a well-buttered shallow casserole dish. Scatter the mushrooms over them and sprinkle with salt and pepper. Mix together the lemon juice, water, sugar and parsley and pour into the casserole dish. Dot with small pieces of butter.

Cover and cook near the top of a preheated oven, 350°F, for 20 minutes. Remove the cover, baste with the juices, cover and cook for 10 minutes. Garnish with fennel leaves.

BRAZIL MUSHROOM CASSEROLE

Serves 4

1 pound chestnut mushrooms
4 tomatoes, sliced
4 scallions, finely chopped
1 tablespoon chopped fresh oregano
or marjoram
1 tablespoon chopped fresh basil
1 teaspoon rosemary leaves
¼ cup dry white wine or stock
1 cup coarsely ground Brazil nuts
1 cup fresh whole wheat bread crumbs
salt and freshly ground black pepper

Arrange the mushrooms, tomatoes and scallions in layers in a casserole dish, sprinkling each layer with the fresh herbs and seasoning to taste. Pour on the wine or stock.

Mix the nuts and bread crumbs together and sprinkle over the top of the casserole. Bake in a preheated oven, 375°F, for 25-30 minutes until the mushrooms are tender and the topping is browned. Serve hot.

MICROWAVE METHOD: Arrange in a casserole dish as above. Cover and cook on High for 10 minutes. Place under a preheated broiler to brown topping.

STIR-FRIED GARLIC MUSHROOMS

Serves 4

2 tablespoons olive oil
1 tablespoon butter
½ pound mixed mushrooms, such as
shiitake and chestnut, rinsed,
trimmed and thickly sliced (*about 2 cups*)
3-4 garlic cloves, crushed
¼ pound oyster mushrooms, rinsed,
trimmed and thickly sliced (*about 1 cup*)
2-3 tablespoons dry sherry or vermouth
4 tablespoons chopped fresh parsley
salt and freshly ground black pepper

Heat a wok or large skillet until hot. Add the olive oil and butter and heat over a moderate heat until foaming. Add the shiitake and chestnut mushrooms, garlic, salt and plenty of pepper. Increase the heat to high and stir-sauté for 2 minutes. Add the oyster mushrooms, sprinkle over the sherry or vermouth and stir-fry for 3 minutes or until the mushrooms are tender.

Taste and adjust the seasoning if necessary, then remove the pan from the heat and stir in the chopped parsley. Serve at once.

Illustrated opposite

BRAISED CHANTERELLES

Serves 6

1 tablespoon butter
6 bacon slices, chopped
1½ pounds chanterelles (*if unavailable, use shiitake or chestnut mushrooms*),
rinsed, trimmed and halved if large
2 teaspoons all-purpose flour
⅔ cup beef stock
½ cup dry red wine
1 parsley sprig, chopped
salt
pinch of cayenne

Melt the butter in a saucepan and cook the bacon until crisp. Remove with a slotted spoon and set aside.

Add the chanterelles to the pan and cook for 5 minutes. Add the flour and cook, stirring, for 1 minute. Gradually stir in the stock and red wine. Season with salt to taste and the cayenne. Return the bacon to the pan and simmer over a low heat for about 10 minutes. Stir in the chopped parsley and serve immediately.

MUSHROOMS WITH GREEN PEPPERCORNS

Serves 4

2 tablespoons olive oil
1 pound medium mushrooms
¼ cup water
1 tablespoon fresh green peppercorns in brine,
lightly crushed (*see note below*)
2 tablespoons heavy cream
salt
croutons, to serve
fresh cilantro leaves or parsley sprigs,
for garnish

Heat the olive oil in a large skillet and sauté the mushrooms quickly for about 5 minutes until just beginning to brown. Add the water and a little salt, cover the pan and simmer for about 10 minutes, by which time there will be a fair amount of liquid in the pan.

Stir the peppercorns and cream into the mushrooms and reheat gently without boiling. Tip into a warm serving dish and scatter with the croutons. Garnish with the cilantro leaves or parsley sprigs and serve immediately as an appetizer or an unusual side dish.

Note: Fresh green peppercorns in brine are available in jars or small cans from delicatessens or large supermarkets. They are quite soft, and so can be crushed easily.

MUSHROOM CURRY

Serves 4

2 onions, chopped
½ stick butter or ¼ cup clarified butter
2 tablespoons tomato paste
1 teaspoon ground cinnamon
½ teaspoon garam masala
½ teaspoon ground cloves
4 cup sliced medium mushrooms
⅔ cup plain yogurt
1¼ cups vegetable stock
¼ teaspoon chili powder
salt and freshly ground black pepper
fresh cilantro leaves, for garnish

Sauté the onions in the butter or clarified butter until golden brown. Add the tomato paste, cinnamon, garam masala and ground cloves and continue cooking, stirring constantly, for 4-5 minutes.

Add the mushrooms and a few drops of water. Cook, stirring for 4-5 minutes. Gradually add the yogurt and cook for a further 3 minutes. Then add the stock and simmer for 15 minutes. Season to taste and add the chili powder.

Serve on a bed of rice, garnished with fresh cilantro leaves.

CEPES WITH HERB SAUCE

Serves 6

3 tablespoons butter
1 garlic clove, halved
1½ pounds cèpes or other wild mushrooms, rinsed, trimmed and cut into bite-size pieces
1 tablespoon chopped fresh parsley
1 tablespoon chopped fresh chervil
1 tablespoon chopped fresh basil
1 tablespoon all-purpose flour
⅓ cup dry white wine
⅔ cup heavy or sour cream
salt and freshly ground white pepper

Melt the butter in a large saucepan. Add the garlic and cook until golden brown. Remove and discard the garlic. Add the cèpes or other wild mushrooms to the pan and cook over a low heat for about 10-15 minutes.

Add half of the chopped herbs to the pan and mix well. Stir in the flour and cook for 2-3 minutes, stirring well. Remove from the heat then gradually add the wine, stirring well after each addition to make a smooth sauce. Bring to a boil while stirring and cook for about 1-2 minutes, until sauce thickens. Mix in the heavy or sour cream and reheat without boiling. Season to taste.

Transfer to a dish, sprinkle with the remaining herbs and serve with French bread.

BAKED MUSHROOMS WITH GARLIC BUTTER

Serves 4

1 pound large mushrooms
grated rind and juice of 1 small lemon
1½ sticks butter, softened
4-5 garlic cloves, crushed
¼ cup dry whole wheat bread crumbs
salt and freshly ground black pepper
chopped fresh parsley, for garnish

Trim the mushroom stems and arrange the mushrooms, stems up, in four well-buttered gratin dishes. Season with the salt, pepper and lemon juice.

Cream the butter with the garlic and lemon rind and work in the dry bread crumbs. Shape into a roll and chill.

Cover the mushrooms with foil and bake in a preheated oven, 400°F, for 5 minutes until only partly cooked.

Cut the garlic butter roll into slices and put one on each mushroom cap. Return mushrooms to the oven until crispy or finish under the broiler.

Garnish the mushrooms with chopped fresh parsley and serve with crusty French bread to mop up the garlic butter.

MORELS WITH WILD RICE

Serves 2

5 ounces fresh morels, rinsed,
trimmed and halved lengthwise,
or ½ ounce dried morels plus ¼ ounce dried
horn of plenty mushrooms and ¼ pound mixed
fresh mushrooms, such as shiitake,
yellow and gray oyster, trimmed
⅔ cup raw wild rice, well rinsed
½ stick butter
6 tablespoons heavy cream
1 tablespoon brandy
salt and freshly ground black pepper

If using dried mushrooms, soak in warm water for 20-30 minutes, then drain. Cook rice in a saucepan of salted boiling water 18-20 minutes until the grains begin to split. Drain well.

Meanwhile, melt half the butter in a heavy-bottom skillet, add all of the mushrooms and sauté over a moderately high heat 2-3 minutes. Season to taste, add the cream and brandy and reduce the heat. Continue cooking until the liquid has almost all evaporated. Transfer mushrooms to a bowl, cover and keep warm.

Melt remaining butter in the pan, add the wild rice and reheat, stirring to coat well. Season to taste and serve topped with the mushrooms.

Illustrated opposite

SPICY MUSHROOMS

Serves 4

3 tablespoons corn oil
1 teaspoon poppy seeds
1 teaspoon sesame seeds
1 teaspoon black mustard seeds
4 tablespoons mild curry paste
⅔ cup plain yogurt
2 teaspoons garam masala
1 tablespoon cumin
1 pound chestnut mushrooms, halved if large
salt
chopped fresh cilantro, for garnish

Heat the oil in a large wok or skillet and stir-fry the poppy, sesame and black mustard seeds for 1 minute. Add the curry paste and stir-fry for 1 minute. Gradually add the yogurt stirring well between each addition. Stir in the garam masala, cumin and salt to taste. Add the mushrooms, stir to coat them in the curry sauce and place the lid on the pan. Cook over a low heat for 10 minutes, serve at once as an appetizer, sprinkled with cilantro.

MICROWAVE METHOD: Place the oil in a large casserole dish and cook on High for 30 seconds. Add the seeds and curry paste. Cook on High for 1 minute. Stir in the yogurt, garam masala, cumin and salt. Cook on High for 1 minute. Add the mushrooms, stir to coat, cover and cook on High for 6-7 minutes. Serve as above.

MUSHROOMS KIEV

Serves 4

24 small mushrooms
1 stick butter, softened
2-3 garlic cloves, crushed
2 tablespoons finely chopped fresh parsley
2 eggs, beaten
¾ cup dry white bread crumbs
corn oil, for deep-frying
salt and freshly ground black pepper
Belgian endive leaves, for garnish

Trim the stems from the mushrooms and chop very finely. Put the softened butter in a bowl with the chopped mushroom stems, garlic, parsley and seasoning to taste. Beat together well. Spoon into the mushroom caps, then sandwich the mushrooms together in pairs, using wooden toothpicks to secure them.

Dip the mushroom pairs one at a time into the beaten egg, then roll in the bread crumbs. Repeat once more. Chill for 1 hour.

Heat the oil in a deep-fat fryer to 375°F, or until a cube of bread browns in 30 seconds. Sauté the mushrooms a few at a time for about 5 minutes, turning frequently with a slotted spoon until golden brown and crisp on all sides. Drain on paper towels and keep hot while cooking the remainder.

Remove toothpicks and serve immediately, garnished with endive leaves.

STUFFED MUSHROOMS

Serves 4-6

1¼ pounds large stuffing mushrooms,
the stems removed and finely chopped,
the caps sprinkled with a little lemon juice
⅔ cup diced carrots
½ cup beef stock
1 tablespoon butter
1 tablespoon all-purpose flour
pinch of ground nutmeg
pinch of curry powder
½ cup chopped cooked ham
⅔ cup cooked shelled shrimps
1 cup diced mild cheese
1 sweet red pepper, cored, seeded and sliced
1 cup grated Parmesan cheese
salt and freshly ground black pepper

Place mushroom caps in greased dish. Bring carrots and stock to boil in a saucepan, then simmer gently 8-10 minutes. Drain, reserving the stock. Melt butter in a pan, stir in flour, cook for 1 minute. Whisk in reserved stock. Season with salt, pepper, nutmeg and curry powder. Add carrots, ham, shrimp, cheese, red pepper and mushroom stems. Bring mixture to boil, stirring constantly. Use to fill mushroom caps. Sprinkle with Parmesan, cook in a preheated oven, 425°F, for about 12 minutes, until golden. Serve immediately.

MUSHROOMS WITH BANANA SAUCE

Serves 4

1 pound medium mushrooms
2 eggs, beaten
about 1 cup dry white bread crumbs
corn oil, for deep-frying

SAUCE:

1 large ripe banana
1 large garlic clove, crushed
3 tablespoons mayonnaise
2 tablespoons light cream
freshly grated nutmeg
paprika
salt and freshly ground black pepper

Trim mushroom stems so the mushrooms are round. Dip mushrooms in the egg and coat in bread crumbs. Chill while preparing the sauce.

Mash bananas and garlic with mayonnaise, then stir in the cream. Add salt and pepper to taste and a little grated nutmeg, then pour the sauce into a serving dish and sprinkle a little paprika over the top. Chill until required.

Heat oil in a deep-fat fryer to 375°F or until a cube of bread browns in 30 seconds. Sauté mushrooms, a few at a time, until coating is crisp and golden, drain on paper towels and keep hot until all are cooked. Serve on a bed of lettuce, with the sauce handed separately. This is delicious as an appetizer.

SPINACH & MUSHROOM ROULADE

Serves 4

1 package (*about 10 ounces*) frozen chopped spinach, thawed, or 1 pound fresh spinach
1 teaspoon butter
4 eggs, separated
¼ cup grated Parmesan cheese
salt and freshly ground black pepper
oakleaf or salad bowl lettuce, for garnish

FILLING:

1 tablespoon butter
1½ cups sliced medium mushrooms
1 tablespoon all-purpose flour
⅔ cup milk
pinch of nutmeg

Line a 12 x 8-inch jelly roll pan with nonstick parchment and then oil lightly, or make a case of the same measurements with aluminum foil.

Place the spinach in a saucepan with the teaspoon of butter and cook until completely softened. Drain the spinach well, chop if fresh and place in a large bowl. Add the egg yolks, beating them well into the chopped spinach and season to taste.

Whisk the egg whites in a large grease-free bowl until just holding their shape. Using a metal spoon, quickly fold them into the spinach mixture. Spoon the mixture into the prepared jelly roll pan, sprinkle the grated Parmesan over the surface, and bake in a preheated oven, 400°F, for 10 minutes.

Meanwhile, make the filling. Heat the butter in a small saucepan. Add the sliced mushrooms and cook gently until softened. Stir in the flour and cook, stirring constantly for an additional 1 minute. Slowly stir in the milk and cook the sauce until thickened. Stir in the nutmeg and seasoning to taste.

Remove the spinach roulade from the oven and invert onto a sheet of waxed paper. Quickly spread the mushroom filling over the surface and gently roll the roulade up. Cut into thick slices and serve immediately with a lettuce garnish.

Illustrated opposite

CRISPY STIR-FRIED MUSHROOMS

Serves 4-6

1 egg
1 egg yolk
½ tablespoon finely chopped parsley
4 cups thickly sliced large mushrooms
5 tablespoons dry white bread crumbs
¼ stick butter
1 garlic clove, halved
salt and freshly ground black pepper

Beat the egg well with the egg yolk and chopped parsley, and season to taste. Dip the mushroom slices in the egg mixture and coat in the dry bread crumbs.

Melt the butter in a large skillet, cook the garlic until golden brown, then remove and discard. Add the mushrooms and quickly stir-fry until golden brown on all sides. Serve immediately with a flavored mayonnaise and crusty French bread.

MUSHROOM FONDUE

Serves 6

¼ stick butter
2 shallots or small onions, finely chopped
1 cup chopped chestnut mushrooms
1¼ cups dry white wine
2 cups shredded Gruyère cheese
2 cups shredded Jarlsberg or Emmentaler cheese
1 tablespoon cornstarch
¼ cup light cream
pinch of dry mustard
freshly ground black pepper

Melt the butter in a fondue pan over a gentle heat. Add the shallots or onions and cook until softened, then add the mushrooms and cook for 2-3 minutes.

Reserve 1 tablespoon of the wine and add the remainder to the fondue pan, heating gently until nearly boiling. Gradually add the shredded cheeses, stirring until melted.

Stir the reserved wine and the cornstarch together and add to the fondue, stirring until thickened. Stir in the cream and add a pinch of dry mustard and pepper to taste.

Serve with grissini and vegetable crudités to dip into the fondue.

STUFFED CHINESE MUSHROOMS

Serves 4

16 large dried Chinese mushrooms
16 cooked shelled shrimp

FILLING:

2 cups lean ground pork
2 tablespoons rich soy sauce
1 tablespoon sesame oil
1-inch piece of fresh ginger, minced

FOR GARNISH:

a few radishes
1 small bunch scallions
watercress sprigs

Place the dried Chinese mushrooms in a bowl and cover with boiling water. Let stand for 30 minutes.

Meanwhile, to prepare the garnish, trim the radishes and cut down through them several times, to give small wedges all attached at the base. Place these radish flowers in a bowl of iced water and place in the refrigerator. To make the ends of the scallions curl, wash them and trim off any limp parts. Leave plenty of the green part on the scallions, then cut down into these to give fine strips, all attached to the white base. Place in iced water with the radishes and leave for at least 45 minutes to curl.

To make the filling for the mushrooms, place the lean ground pork in a large bowl. Add the rich soy sauce, sesame oil and minced ginger, mixing well to ensure that all of the filling ingredients are thoroughly combined.

Drain the soaked mushrooms and divide the filling equally among eight of them, then press the remaining eight mushrooms on top. Press the mushrooms well together between the palms of your hands, holding them over a plate as you do this because a little water may be squeezed out.

Place the stuffed mushrooms on a deep plate with a rim or in a shallow dish and stand it on the steaming rack in a wok. Pour in enough water to come up to the level of the rack and bring to a boil, then reduce the heat and simmer rapidly, with the lid on the wok, for 20 minutes.

Place two shelled shrimp on top of each mushroom, re-cover the wok and simmer for a further 5 minutes.

To serve, transfer the mushrooms to a heated serving dish and pour a little of the liquid from the plate over them. Garnish each mushroom with a tiny sprig of watercress placed between the shrimp, and arrange the scallion curls between and around the mushrooms on the plate. Serve immediately.

MUSHROOM & PEPPER PIZZA

Serves 4

TOPPING:

2 tablespoons corn oil

2 medium onions, sliced

1 can (*about 14 ounces*) chopped tomatoes

2 tablespoons tomato paste

⅔ cup shredded mozzarella cheese

½ sweet red pepper, cored, seeded and sliced

½ sweet orange pepper, cored, seeded and sliced

½ sweet green pepper, cored, seeded and sliced

1 garlic clove, crushed

1 cup sliced mixed mushrooms, such as
oyster, shiitake and chestnut

salt and freshly ground black pepper

DOUGH:

2 cups bread flour

½ teaspoon salt

1 package rapid-rise active dry yeast

pinch of sugar

⅔ cup tepid water

To make the pizza dough, sift the flour with the salt into a large bowl. Stir in the yeast and sugar. Make a depression in the center of the flour and pour in the warm water. Beat with a wooden spoon until it all clings together, adding more water if required, then tip out the dough onto a floured surface and knead for 10 minutes, or until smooth.

Place the dough in a lightly oiled clean bowl and cover the bowl with plastic wrap. Stand the bowl in a warm place for 30-60 minutes until the dough has roughly doubled in bulk.

When the dough has risen sufficiently, punch it down and tip it out on to a floured board. Knead again briefly for 2-3 minutes. Roll out to a 10-inch circle and carefully transfer to a large greased baking sheet.

To make the topping, heat half the oil in a skillet, add the onions and cook gently until softened. Mix with the chopped tomatoes, tomato paste and seasoning. Spread over the dough base. Sprinkle with half the mozzarella and cook in a preheated oven, 425°F, for 15 minutes. Sauté the sliced peppers in the remaining oil with the garlic and mushrooms for 5 minutes.

Arrange the peppers and mushrooms over the pizza. Sprinkle with the remaining mozzarella and return to the oven for 10 minutes or until the base is cooked. Serve with crusty bread and a green salad.

Illustrated opposite

MUSHROOM RAVIOLI

Serves 4

FILLING:

1 onion, finely chopped

1-2 garlic cloves, crushed

2 tablespoons olive oil

4 cups finely chopped chestnut mushrooms

1 cup ricotta cheese

1 egg, beaten

2-3 tablespoons fresh white bread crumbs

¾ stick butter

½ cup grated Parmesan cheese

salt and freshly ground black pepper

EGG PASTA DOUGH:

4 cups bread flour

good pinch of salt

4 eggs

1 teaspoon olive oil

1-2 tablespoons water

To make the pasta dough, sift the flour and salt into a bowl. Make a hollow in the center, drop in the eggs and oil. Draw the flour into the center, add 1-2 tablespoons of water if the mixture is too dry – the finished dough should be fairly firm to the touch. Knead the dough until smooth and elastic; this is essential if the dough is to roll properly. Wrap the dough closely and leave to rest for a minimum of 15 minutes and a maximum of 2 hours.

Working quickly, roll out the dough with a rolling pin, giving the dough a quarter turn between each roll, until it measures 8-9 inches in diameter. Now work on the dough, rolling and stretching it until it is paper thin and has been stretched to a square measuring about 16-18inches long. Cut out 2½-inch rounds.

For the filling, cook the onion and garlic gently in the oil until soft and lightly colored. Add the mushrooms and continue to cook gently until the mushrooms are soft and any liquid has evaporated. Remove from the heat, beat in the ricotta and egg and sufficient bread crumbs to give a firm mixture. Season. Place a little mixture on each dough round, brush around the edge with cold water, fold over and seal to make half-moon shapes.

Cook a few ravioli at a time for 4-5 minutes in salted boiling water. They are cooked when they rise to the surface. Remove with a slotted spoon, drain well and place in a serving dish. Cover and keep hot until all the ravioli are cooked. Just before serving, heat the butter in a pan until it is a light golden brown and pour immediately over the ravioli. Sprinkle a little of the Parmesan over and serve the rest separately. Serve the ravioli hot.

MUSHROOM LASAGNE

Serves 4

1 large onion, chopped
2 tablespoons olive oil
2 cups sliced medium mushrooms
1 tablespoon all-purpose flour
1 tablespoon lemon juice
2½ cups plain yogurt
¾ cup chopped walnuts
2 slices (*about 4 ounces*) lean ham,
cut in julienne strips
1 tablespoon fresh chopped parsley
9 no pre-cook lasagne sheets
1½ cups shredded Cheddar cheese
6 tablespoons fresh whole wheat bread crumbs
salt and freshly ground black pepper

Sauté onion in the oil for 3 minutes, add mushrooms and cook for 2 minutes. Stir in flour, cook for 1 minute. Remove from heat and stir in lemon juice and half the yogurt. Cook, stirring, over low heat until mixture thickens, season. Simmer for 2 minutes. Stir in walnuts, ham and parsley and remove from the heat. Pour some of mixture into a greased baking dish. Cover with sheets of lasagne and continue making layers, finishing with lasagne.

Combine remaining yogurt and half the cheese, pouring over lasagne. Sprinkle over bread crumbs and remaining cheese. Bake on baking tray in a preheated oven, 375°F, for 25-30 minutes, or until golden brown.

FARFALLE WITH MUSHROOMS

Serves 4

2-2½ cups farfalle (*pasta bows*)
¼ stick butter
2 tablespoons olive oil
4 cups small button mushrooms
2 garlic cloves, crushed
1 can (*2 ounces*) anchovies in oil,
drained and coarsely chopped
6 tablespoons fresh chopped parsley
1¼ cups sour cream
salt and freshly ground black pepper

Cook the pasta in a large saucepan of salted boiling water for 10 minutes, or according to the package directions, stirring occasionally.

Melt butter and oil in a heavy-bottom saucepan. Add mushrooms and garlic and sauté over a moderate heat, for 5 minutes until juices flow from the mushrooms.

Add the anchovies and season with pepper to taste. Cook for a further 5 minutes. Remove the saucepan from the heat and stir in 4 tablespoons of the parsley and the cream. Heat gently but do not boil.

Drain the pasta and tip into a warm bowl. Add the sauce and toss gently. Sprinkle with the remaining parsley and serve.

MUSHROOM PASTA WITH PIGNOLI

Serves 4

1½ tablespoons corn oil

1 onion, sliced

5 cups sliced large mushrooms

1-2 teaspoons fresh green peppercorns
in brine (*see page 30*)

1 tablespoon soy sauce

3 tablespoons water

2 tablespoons heavy cream

3 cups pasta shapes
(*quills, spirals or cartwheels*)

2 tablespoons pignoli (*pine nuts*)

salt

1 tablespoon chopped fresh parsley, for garnish

Heat 1 tablespoon of the corn oil in a large saucepan. Add the sliced onion to the oil and sauté for about 5 minutes. Add the sliced mushrooms to the pan and cook for a further few minutes until they have cooked down a little.

Add salt to taste, the green peppercorns, soy sauce and water. Cover the saucepan and simmer gently for 15 minutes, then remove the lid and cook quickly for 3-4 minutes to reduce some of the liquid.

Pour the mushroom mixture into a blender or food processor and blend very briefly, for just a few seconds (the mushrooms should retain some texture). Return to the rinsed pan and stir in the heavy cream.

Prepare the pasta. Bring a large pan of lightly salted water to a boil. Add the pasta to the water, stir a couple of times and boil briskly for 10 minutes, or according to package directions. Drain thoroughly.

Meanwhile, heat the remaining oil in a small saucepan and sauté the pignoli for just 30 seconds until golden brown. Drain them on paper towels and set aside.

To serve, reheat the mushroom sauce without boiling and pour over the cooked pasta. Sprinkle with the browned pignoli and chopped parsley and serve immediately.

Illustrated opposite

CRISPY NOODLES WITH MUSHROOMS & HAM

Serves 4

5 cups lightly salted boiling water
¾ pound chow mein noodles
(*thin Chinese egg noodles*)
½ stick butter
2 tablespoons corn oil
½ pound oyster mushrooms
½ pound cooked ham, shredded
1 bunch of scallions, finely chopped

Pour the boiling water into a wok and add the noodles. Put the lid on the wok and simmer for about 5 minutes; when cooked the noodles should be tender but not sticky. Drain the noodles and place them on a plate, patting them into a round shape.

Heat the butter and 1 tablespoon of the oil together in the wok and add the mushrooms, ham and scallions. Cook for a few minutes, then remove with a slotted spoon. Set aside and keep warm.

Slide the noodles into the wok, adding a little more oil if necessary, and cook over a high heat until golden and crisp underneath, then turn them over and cook the second side in the same way. Sprinkle the ham mixture over the noodles and serve immediately.

YANGCHOW FRIED RICE

Serves 4

3 dried Chinese mushrooms
¼ cup corn oil
2 onions, finely sliced
2 slices of fresh ginger, peeled and diced
½ cup ground pork
1 tablespoon light soy sauce
1 teaspoon sugar
4 cups cooked long-grain rice
2 eggs, beaten
2 tablespoons cooked green peas
2 tomatoes, chopped
salt and freshly ground black pepper

Place the mushrooms in a bowl, cover with boiling water and leave to soak for 20 minutes. Drain, discard the stems and chop.

Heat 3 tablespoons of oil in a large wok or skillet. Add the onions and ginger and stir-fry 1 minute. Add pork and stir-fry for 3 minutes. Add ½ teaspoon salt, soy sauce and sugar and stir-fry for 1 minute. Add the rice to the wok and heat through, turning and stirring well.

Meanwhile, heat remaining oil in a skillet. Season the eggs, add to pan and stir and turn gently. As soon as they have set, add the peas, tomatoes and mushrooms. Stir for 1 minute, then turn egg mixture into the wok containing the rice. Mix lightly together and serve.

MUSHROOM & RAISIN PILAF

Serves 4

¼ **stick butter**
1 tablespoon corn oil
1 large onion, finely chopped
1 garlic clove, crushed
1¼ cups long-grain brown rice
1 cup thinly sliced mushrooms
½ teaspoon dried dill
½ teaspoon turmeric
2½ cups chicken stock
⅓ cup raisins
salt and freshly ground black pepper

FOR GARNISH:

baked cherry tomatoes
cooked broccoli flowerets

Heat the butter and corn oil together in a shallow, flameproof casserole dish over a low heat. Add the finely chopped onion and crushed garlic to the casserole and cook them gently for 3-4 minutes until they are tender and lightly browned.

Add the long-grain brown rice, sliced mushrooms, dill and turmeric to the onion and garlic in the casserole dish and continue cooking for 1-2 minutes, stirring all the time.

Gradually stir the chicken stock into the casserole dish and, if necessary, season lightly with salt and black pepper to taste.

Cover the casserole dish closely with a lid or foil and place on the middle shelf of a preheated oven, 350°F. Cook for 45 minutes, then stir in the raisins. Cover the casserole dish once more and return to the oven for another 10 minutes, or until all of the stock has been absorbed.

Remove the casserole from the oven and transfer the pilaf to a hot serving dish, using a fork to keep the grains of rice separate.

Garnish with baked cherry tomatoes and broccoli flowerets and serve the pilaf as a light meal or as a side dish.

MICROWAVE METHOD: Place butter and oil in a casserole dish. Add onion and garlic and cook on High for 2 minutes. Add the rice, mushrooms, dill, turmeric and hot stock seasoning. Cover and cook on High for 15 minutes. Add raisins and cook on High for 5 minutes then Medium for 15 minutes or until rice is just tender. Serve as above.

FLAKY MUSHROOM ROLL

Serves 4-6

¼ stick butter or margarine
1 onion, chopped
2 cups chopped chestnut mushrooms
2 tablespoons chopped fresh parsley
½ cup brown rice, cooked
1 package (*about 8 ounces*) frozen
puff pastry, thawed
egg yolk, to glaze
salt and freshly ground black pepper

Heat the butter or margarine in a large saucepan and sauté the onion and mushrooms quickly over a high heat for 4-5 minutes. Remove from the heat, stir in the parsley, rice and seasoning and leave to cool.

Roll the pastry into a 13 x 11-inch rectangle. Cut into two strips: 6 x 11-inches and 7 x 11-inches. Place the smaller rectangle on a baking sheet, spoon the mushroom mixture on top, brush the edges with cold water. Fold second piece of pastry in half lengthwise and, using a sharp knife, cut diagonal slits about 1 inch apart in the fold to within 1 inch of the edge. Unfold and place carefully on top of the filling, pressing the edges together; trim and decorate. Brush with egg yolk and bake in a preheated oven, 425°F, for 20-25 minutes until golden. Serve with sour cream and a fresh herb sauce.

WILD MUSHROOM FEUILLETE

Serves 6

1 large package (*about 1 pound*) frozen puff
pastry, thawed
1 tablespoon butter or margarine
4 cups sliced medium white mushroom
3 cups sliced oyster mushrooms
1¼ cups sour cream
1¼ cups light cream
1 garlic clove, crushed
salt and freshly ground black pepper

Roll out the pastry to about ⅛-inch thick and cut out six 5-inch circles and six 3-inch ones. Place circles on a baking sheet, bake in a preheated oven, 450°F, for 10-12 minutes, until puffed up and golden brown.

Meanwhile, melt the butter or margarine and cook the white mushrooms for 3 minutes, add the oyster mushrooms and cook for 2 minutes, until tender. Remove the mushrooms with a slotted spoon and boil the remaining liquid rapidly until reduced to 1 tablespoon. Add the mushrooms, sour and light cream, garlic and seasoning. Reheat gently without boiling.

To serve, place some mushroom mixture and liquid on top of each large pastry circle. Cover each with a smaller pastry circle and serve.

Illustrated opposite

MUSHROOM & MIXED PEPPER QUICHE

Serves 6-8

3 tablespoons butter or margarine
1 small onion, finely chopped
2 cups sliced medium mushrooms
1 small sweet green pepper, cored, seeded
and sliced
1 small sweet red pepper, cored, seeded
and sliced
2 teaspoons lemon juice
3 eggs
1¼ cups light cream
¼ teaspoon ground nutmeg
1 cup shredded Swiss cheese
salt and freshly ground black pepper

DOUGH:

1½ cups all-purpose flour
pinch of salt
¾ stick butter or margarine,
cut into small pieces
1½-2 tablespoons water

To make the dough, sift the flour and salt into a bowl, cut in the butter and rub in until the mixture resembles fine bread crumbs. Add enough water to form a firm dough. Knead lightly until smooth and free from cracks.

Roll out the dough on a lightly floured work surface to a round large enough to line the base and sides of a 8-9-inch loose-based fluted pie pan.

Bake as follows. Line the pie shell with waxed paper and cover with a layer of dry beans to prevent the base from blistering. Place in a preheated oven, 400°F, for 15-20 minutes until the sides of the flan are set and golden. Remove lining paper and beans (which can be reused) and return pie shell to oven for about 5 minutes or until the base is crisp. Let cool.

Melt the butter or margarine in a skillet. Add the onion, mushrooms and peppers and sauté until the onion is softened. Sprinkle with lemon juice and stir. Remove the vegetables with a slotted spoon and arrange in the bottom of the cooked pie shell.

Beat the eggs, cream, nutmeg and salt and pepper together. Pour into the pie shell and sprinkle the top with the cheese.

Bake the quiche in a preheated oven, 425°F, for 10 minutes. Reduce the heat to 350°F, and bake for 15-20 minutes longer or until set. Serve hot or cold with a crisp green salad.

Illustrated on pages 2-3

BRIOCHE WITH MUSHROOMS

Serves 4

butter and all-purpose flour, for coating
1 stick butter
4 large shallots or small onions, finely chopped
1 garlic clove, finely chopped
3 cups sliced medium mushrooms
2 teaspoons brandy
1 cup heavy cream
½ teaspoon chopped fresh chervil
salt and freshly ground black pepper

BRIOCHE DOUGH:

1½ cups all-purpose flour
1 package rapid-rise active dry yeast
pinch of salt
1 teaspoon sugar
¾ stick butter
1-2 tablespoons warm milk
2 eggs

To make the brioche, mix the flour, yeast, salt and sugar together in a large bowl. Melt half of the butter in a pan, stir in 1 tablespoon of the milk and the eggs. Add to the flour and beat well until the dough is smooth and elastic. Add the remaining milk if the dough is too stiff. Work the remaining butter, a little at a time, into the dough. Place the dough in a clean bowl, cover with waxed paper and leave to rise in a warm place for 1-1½ hours, until doubled in bulk.

Knead the dough well on a lightly floured surface and punch down lightly to knock out the air. Cut a quarter from the dough.

Lightly butter four baba molds or similar pans (as a last resort one larger mold will do), dust with flour and shake out the excess. Divide the large piece of dough into four. Knead into round balls and place in the prepared pans. Make a cross in the center of each piece of dough with a knife. Divide the remaining dough into four and roll into pear shapes. Place the thinner end of each in the cross. Brush with beaten egg and bake in a preheated oven, 400°F, for 20-25 minutes.

Melt the butter in a saucepan, add the shallots or onions and garlic and cook for a few minutes. Add the mushrooms and cook for a further few minutes. Season to taste, then stir in the brandy and cream. Reduce over a moderate heat until the cream coats the back of a spoon. Check the seasoning and add the chopped fresh chervil.

When the brioches are cooked, remove from the molds. With the point of a knife, cut a "lid" from the top of each brioche. Remove some of the dough and divide the mushroom mixture among the brioches. Replace the lids and return to the oven for about 2 minutes to warm through.

Note: If you don't have time to make your own brioches you can buy them ready-made.

MUSHROOM & ONION PIE

Serves 4-6

3 tablespoons butter
1 onion, chopped
1 cup small onions
1 pound small mushrooms
1 tablespoon finely chopped fresh parsley
2 tablespoons sherry or Madeira
1 cup heavy cream
2 egg yolks, beaten
¼ teaspoon freshly grated nutmeg
¼ teaspoon paprika
1 package (*8 ounces*) frozen puff pastry, thawed
salt and freshly ground black pepper
beaten egg white, for glazing

Melt the butter in a large skillet. Add the chopped onion and small onions and cook, shaking the pan occasionally, over a low heat for 5 minutes.

Add the whole mushrooms to the skillet, turning them gently so that they are well coated with the butter. Stir in the chopped fresh parsley, season with salt and pepper to taste and cook for 2 minutes.

Using a slotted spoon, transfer the onions and mushrooms to a deep pie dish.

Increase the heat, pour the sherry or Madeira into the skillet and stir well to mix. Remove the skillet from the heat and pour the contents over the mushrooms and onions.

In a small bowl, combine the heavy cream and the egg yolks. Season with the nutmeg, paprika and a little salt. Pour the mixture into the pie dish.

Roll out the puff pastry, and use to cover the pie, dampening the edges of the dish with water to make the pastry stick. Flute the edge of the pie with the back of a sharp knife to form scallop shapes. Make a slit in the center of the pie crust to let the steam escape.

Brush the pie crust with egg white and bake in a preheated oven, 400°F, for 30 minutes, or until the pastry has risen and is golden brown. Serve the pie immediately with a selection of green vegetables or a mixed salad.

Illustrated opposite

EGG FOO YOUNG

Serves 4

2 dried Chinese mushrooms, or ½ cup chopped
fresh oyster mushrooms
¼ cup finely chopped shelled shrimp
¼ cup finely chopped cooked ham
¼ cup finely chopped bamboo shoots
2-3 water chestnuts, finely chopped
4 eggs, beaten
1 tablespoon cornstarch
¼ cup water
1 teaspoon salt
1 tablespoon dry sherry
3 tablespoons corn oil
fresh cilantro sprigs, for garnish

If using the dried mushrooms, soak in warm
water for about 20 minutes, then squeeze dry,
discard the hard stems and finely chop.

Mix the mushrooms, shrimp, ham, bamboo
shoots and water chestnuts with the beaten
eggs. Add the cornstarch, water, salt and
sherry to the egg mixture and stir.

Heat the oil in a wok or skillet until smoking,
then pour in the egg mixture and scramble
with a fork until the mixture sets. Serve hot,
garnished with cilantro.

CHEESE & MUSHROOM SOUFFLÉS

Serves 4

½ stick butter
1½ cups finely chopped medium mushrooms
½ cup all-purpose flour
1¼ cups milk
3 eggs, separated
2 tablespoons chopped fresh parsley
¾ cup finely shredded Edam cheese
½ teaspoon prepared mustard
salt and freshly ground black pepper

Melt half the butter in a saucepan, add the
mushrooms and cook for 3-4 minutes, until
tender. Place the remaining butter, flour and
milk in another saucepan and heat, whisking
constantly, until the sauce thickens. Cook for
2 minutes.

Cool slightly, then beat in the egg yolks,
mushrooms, parsley, cheese and mustard, and
season to taste.

Whisk the egg whites until stiff and fold into
the mixture. Divide among four individual
greased soufflé dishes. Place in a preheated
oven, 375°F, for 20-25 minutes or until well
risen and golden brown. Serve immediately.

MUSHROOM & BACON KABOBS

Serves 4

12 slices bacon
1 tablespoon Dijon mustard
24 medium mushrooms, trimmed
8 bay leaves

Cut the bacon slices in half and spread each piece with a little mustard. Wrap each mushroom in a piece of bacon, then thread them onto four metal skewers, adding two bay leaves to each skewer.

Cook under a hot broiler, turning once, until the bacon is crisp and brown.

Serve with warmed French bread and a fresh green salad.

CHICKEN WITH MUSHROOMS

Serves 4

4 chicken quarters
dried oregano and ground paprika,
for seasoning
2 tablespoons olive oil
1 tablespoon all-purpose flour
1 pound medium mushrooms, quartered
1¼ cups chicken stock
½ onion, grated
1 sweet green pepper, cored, seeded
and cut into fine strips
⅔ cup heavy cream
¼ cup Cognac
cayenne (*optional*)
salt and freshly ground black pepper

Season the chicken quarters with salt, pepper, oregano and paprika to taste. Heat the oil in a saucepan. Add the chicken and cook until golden brown on all sides. Remove with a slotted spoon. Add the flour and mushrooms and cook for 1-2 minutes. Stir in the chicken stock, onion and green pepper. Return the chicken to the pan. Cover, simmer, over a low heat, for about 30 minutes, until the chicken is tender, stirring occasionally.

About 10 minutes before the end of the cooking time stir in the cream and Cognac. Season to taste with a little more salt and cayenne, if you like. Serve immediately.

WARM TURKEY & MIXED MUSHROOM SALAD

Serves 4

1 small head chicory, leaves separated
1 small head Italian red lettuce, leaves
separated
3 tablespoons olive oil
2-3 bacon slices, chopped
1 pound turkey breast fillets,
cut into thin strips across the grain
¼ pound mixed mushrooms, such as shiitake,
chestnut, yellow and gray oyster,
trimmed and sliced if large
¼ cup lemon juice
salt and freshly ground black pepper

DRESSING:

¼ cup olive oil
2 tablespoon wine vinegar (*red or white*)
1 garlic clove, crushed
1 teaspoon Dijon mustard
pinch of sugar

First prepare the dressing: put all the ingredients into a bowl and whisk well to combine. Put to one side.

Put the chicory and lettuce leaves in a large salad bowl, tearing them into bite-size pieces if you like.

Heat a wok until hot. Add 1 tablespoon of the oil and heat over a moderate heat until hot. Add the bacon and stir-fry for 3-4 minutes or until crisp. Remove the wok from the heat and transfer the bacon to paper towels with a slotted spoon. Leave to drain.

Return the wok to the heat, add another 1 tablespoon of the oil and heat until hot. Add the turkey strips, increase the heat to high and stir-fry for 3-4 minutes or until lightly colored on all sides. Remove the wok from the heat and tip the turkey and its juices into a bowl. Keep hot.

Return the wok to a moderate heat, add the remaining oil and heat until hot. Add the mushrooms, lemon juice and salt and pepper to taste, increase the heat to high and stir-fry until all the liquid has evaporated. Tip the contents of the wok into the bowl with the turkey and toss to combine.

Pour the dressing into the wok and stir until hot and sizzling. Quickly add the turkey and mushroom mixture to the bowl of lettuce, pour over the sizzling dressing and toss quickly to combine. Taste for seasoning and serve at once, sprinkled with the crispy bacon.

Illustrated opposite

BEEF & MUSHROOMS IN RED WINE

Serves 4

2 cups sliced large mushrooms
1 tablespoon corn oil
3 tablespoons butter
1 onion, chopped
1½ pounds top round of beef,
cut into thin strips
2 tablespoons all-purpose flour
½ teaspoon mixed dried herbs
1 garlic clove, crushed
1 tablespoon port
⅔ cup beef stock
⅔ cup red wine
salt and freshly ground black pepper

Sauté the mushrooms in oil and butter for 2 minutes over a moderate heat, then remove. Sauté the onion for 3-4 minutes, stirring once or twice.

Toss the beef in flour mixed with salt, pepper and dried herbs. Shake off the excess flour and add the meat to the pan. Sauté for 5 minutes, stirring frequently. Stir in the crushed garlic, the mushrooms, port, stock and wine and bring the sauce to a boil. Reduce heat, cover and simmer for 25 minutes. Taste the sauce and adjust seasoning, if necessary. Serve with boiled new potatoes and fresh vegetables.

NEAPOLITAN PORK CHOPS

Serves 4

2 tablespoons olive oil
1 garlic clove, crushed
4 thick center-cut pork chops
¼ cup white wine
3 tablespoons tomato paste
1 sweet green pepper, cored, seeded and chopped
½ pound small mushrooms, quartered
salt and freshly ground black pepper

Heat the olive oil in a large skillet and sauté the garlic until brown. Discard the garlic. Add the pork chops and sauté on both sides until brown. Season the chops with a sprinkling of salt and pepper.

Mix the white wine and tomato paste together and add to the pan. Add the green pepper and mushrooms and cook, covered, over a low heat for 30 minutes or until the chops are cooked. Transfer to a warm serving plate and serve immediately.

LEMON FRIED FISH WITH MUSHROOMS & SNOW PEAS

Serves 3-4

**4 pompano fillets, skinned
and cut into bite-size pieces
2 tablespoons corn oil
2 tablespoons sesame oil
2 cups sliced oyster mushrooms
½ pound snow peas, prepared for cooking
flat-leaf parsley sprigs, for garnish**

MARINADE:

**1-inch piece of fresh ginger,
peeled and minced
1 garlic clove, crushed
3 tablespoons soy sauce
finely grated rind and juice of 1 large lemon
½ teaspoon five-spice powder**

To make the marinade, place the minced ginger and crushed garlic in a shallow dish with the soy sauce, lemon rind, lemon juice and five-spice powder and combine well.

Add the pieces of pompano to the dish and turn to coat thoroughly in the marinade. Cover the dish and leave to marinate for about 30 minutes, turning the fish over occasionally.

Heat a wok or large skillet until hot. Add 1 tablespoon each of the corn and sesame oil and heat over a moderate heat until hot. Add the sliced mushrooms and prepared snow peas and stir-fry for 3-4 minutes. Tip the contents of the wok or skillet into a bowl and set aside.

Return the wok or skillet to the heat, add the remaining corn and sesame oil and heat until hot. With a slotted spoon, lift the pompano pieces out of the marinade and place carefully in the pan.

Stir-fry the fish pieces for 5 minutes, then return the mushrooms and snow peas to the wok or skillet with their juices and pour in the marinade.

Increase the heat to high and gently toss until all the ingredients are combined and piping hot. Serve at once, garnished with sprigs of flat-leaf parsley.

TROUT & MOREL CREAM SAUCE

Serves 4

2 tablespoons dried morel mushrooms, soaked
in warm water for 20 minutes, then drained
4 trout, about 6 ounces each,
drawn and cleaned
¼ cup lemon juice
1 bunch mixed herbs: parsley, chives, thyme
1¼ cups water
1¼ cups dry white wine
2 juniper berries, crushed
2 black peppercorns, crushed
2 teaspoons cornstarch
⅔ cup heavy cream
pat of butter
salt and freshly ground white pepper

Sprinkle fish with lemon juice, leave 5 minutes. Season fish, inside and out, with salt and
pepper. Stuff each fish with whole herb sprigs.

Heat water and wine in a saucepan with a
scant ½ teaspoon of salt until almost boiling.
Add the trout and morels, reduce the heat and
simmer for 10-15 minutes, turning the fish
once. Transfer trout to a dish; keep warm. Stir
juniper berries and peppercorns into pan. Boil
stock 2-3 minutes to reduce to about 1¼ cups.
Mix the cornstarch and a little water to a thin
paste, whisk into the stock, blend well and
cook, stirring, 1-2 minutes. Stir in cream and
butter. Pour sauce over trout and serve.

JUMBO SHRIMP WITH MUSHROOMS

Serves 4

20 raw jumbo shrimp
1 tablespoon seasoned flour
1 tablespoon corn oil
¼ stick butter
2 shallots or 1 small onion, finely chopped
1 large garlic clove, crushed
½ pound mushrooms, quartered
2 tablespoons lemon juice
3 tablespoons chopped fresh parsley (*optional*)
salt and freshly ground black pepper

Wash the shrimp and shell carefully, leaving
the tails intact. Pat the shrimp dry with paper
towels and toss in the seasoned flour.

Heat the oil and butter in a skillet, add the
shallots or onion and cook gently for 5 minutes.
Stir in the garlic and cook for 1 minute.

Add the shrimp and mushrooms and cook
gently for 5-6 minutes, stirring frequently. Stir
in the lemon juice and the parsley, if using.
Adjust the seasoning to taste and serve with
crusty bread to mop up the juices.

Illustrated opposite

MARINATED MUSHROOMS

Serves 4

1 tablespoon cider vinegar
1 tablespoon olive oil
1 tablespoon lemon juice
few drops of Worcestershire sauce
2 tablespoons tomato paste
2 tablespoons cold water
1 tablespoon chopped fresh mixed herbs,
or ½ tablespoon dried
1 small onion, minced
1 garlic clove, crushed
4 cups sliced mushrooms

Place all the ingredients, except the mushrooms, in a large screw-top jar and shake well. Add the mushrooms, pushing them down if necessary. Shake the jar once again, so the mushrooms are coated with the marinade. Any covered container may be used if you don't have a large screw-top jar.

Stand the jar in a cool place and leave for 24 hours, shaking occasionally so that the mushrooms soften. They will reduce in bulk considerably during this time and also produce quite a lot of liquid.

Serve chilled with French bread.

MUSHROOM STUFFING

Serves 4

¼ stick butter
1 cup finely chopped large mushrooms,
1 small onion, chopped
1½ cups fresh white bread crumbs
2 tablespoons lemon juice
1 teaspoon chopped fresh parsley
2 egg yolks, beaten
salt and freshly ground black pepper

Melt the butter in a saucepan and cook the mushrooms and onion for 3-4 minutes. Add the fresh bread crumbs, lemon juice, chopped parsley, salt and pepper. Mix well and bind the mixture together with the egg yolks.

Use the stuffing for fish fillets or as an accompaniment to ham.

MUSHROOM KETCHUP

Makes about 5 cups

2 pounds large mushrooms, chopped
4 tablespoons salt
1 tablespoon ground allspice
1 small piece of fresh ginger, coarsely chopped
ground nutmeg
1 shallot or 1 small onion, finely chopped
2½ cups red wine vinegar

Layer the mushrooms and salt in a lidded jar. Cover, leave 2 days, stirring four times. Place in a saucepan with the remaining ingredients. Cover, simmer 30 minutes. Pour through fine strainer, pressing gently to extract all the juice. Pour into hot sterilized screw-top bottles or bottling jars which *must* then be sterilized as follows to prevent fermenting: screw tops on loosely. Place bottles in deep pan, completely immerse in cold water while standing on a base of wire, wood or cloth – they will crack if they touch the bottom of the pan. Separate from each other with a cloth. Cover, heat the water, keep it at 170°F for 30 minutes, or at 190°F for 20 minutes. Remove bottles, place on a wooden surface to prevent them from cracking. Tighten screw bands at once.

Leave 24 hours, test for a seal: remove screw-band, grip lid only with your fingers. If lid stays firm, a vacuum has been created; replace screwband. If lid comes away, use at once. As long as seal stays intact ketchup is safe to eat.

MUSHROOM SAUCE

Makes 1¼ cups

½ cup sliced medium mushrooms
3 tablespoons butter
1 teaspoon lemon juice
¼ cup all-purpose flour
1¼ cups milk
salt and freshly ground black pepper

Sauté the sliced mushrooms in 1 tablespoon of the butter with the lemon juice for 5 minutes.

Meanwhile, melt the remaining butter in a small saucepan, stir in the flour and cook, stirring, for 1 minute. Remove from the heat and gradually beat in the milk, and salt and pepper to taste. Return to the heat, bring to a boil and cook for 2 minutes, stirring constantly.

Remove from the heat. Stir the sautéed mushrooms into the finished white sauce and serve with fish, meat or vegetable dishes.

MICROWAVE METHOD: Place 1 tablespoon butter and the mushrooms in a small bowl and cook on High for 2 minutes. Set aside. Place remaining butter in a medium bowl and cook on High for 30 seconds or until melted. Stir in flour and cook on High for 30 seconds. Gradually stir in milk and lemon juice. Season. Cook on High for 3 minutes, or until thickened, beating 3-4 times. Finish as above.

THE MUSHROOM INDEX